Changing Shape

Tales from Ovid's *Metamorphoses*

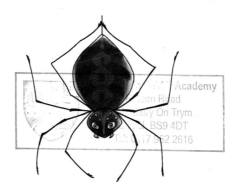

Original stories by Ovid
Retold by Gillian Cross
Series Advisor Professor Kimberley Reynolds
Illustrated by Amerigo Pinelli

OXFORD
UNIVERSITY PRESS

Letter from the Author

I love stories. When I was a
child, I used to climb a tree
in our garden and sit up there
reading. I made up my own
stories too, and told them to my

friends on the way to school.
When I was twenty-eight, I
finally wrote a book – and I haven't stopped
since. I've written over fifty. When I'm not
reading or writing, I love taking photos
and orienteering.

Some of the most magical tales are
about people who change into other things,
like birds, or trees. Long ago, a Roman
writer called Ovid collected over two
hundred of them in a *massive* poem called
Metamorphoses. Three of his best stories are
in this book.

Gillian Cross

Echo and Narcissus[1]

Echo was a wood nymph who lived in the forest. She *loved* talking.

She talked to farmers and hunters. She talked to children out playing and old men picking mushrooms. She chattered to everyone, on and on and on. Once she started, it was hard to get away.

[1] say 'nar-sis-us'

Then she made a terrible mistake. She
started chattering to Juno, the Queen of the
gods. And Juno lost her temper.

'Be quiet!' she shouted. 'You're wasting
my time. From now on, you will stop talking
– for ever.'

' ... for ever?' whispered Echo.

'For ever,' Juno said. 'You won't be able to say anything – except other people's last words.'

' ... last words,' Echo whispered.

'That's right,' Juno nodded. 'Unless someone else speaks, you will be silent.'

' ... silent,' Echo murmured sadly, drifting away through the trees.

What could she do? She tried to tell her friends what Juno had done, but she had no words of her own. In the end, she gave up.

She wandered deep into the forest,
hiding in caves and lonely places.
Whenever she heard voices,
she called back, repeating
their last words. But no one
ever answered her.

And then, one day,
she saw Narcissus out
hunting. And she
fell in love with him.

Everyone fell in love with Narcissus. He was sixteen and he was amazingly beautiful. But he never fell in love with anyone himself. He was much too proud.

What he liked was hunting. When Echo first saw him, he and his friends were in the forest, setting traps for deer.

Echo fell in love instantly and – of course – she wanted to speak to Narcissus. But that was impossible.

She followed him through the forest, hiding in bushes and waiting for someone else to speak. She was hoping that Narcissus or one of his friends would say words that she could repeat.

But they never did. Day after day, Echo ran after the hunters, until her heart was breaking.

Then, one day, Narcissus wandered away from his friends. When he realized he was lost, he began to shout.

'Hello! Where have you gone?' he yelled. 'I'm over here!'

' ... over here!' Echo said joyfully. At last! Her chance had come!

Narcissus heard her voice and he thought it was one of his friends, shouting back to him. He came walking towards the bush where Echo was hiding.

'Where are you?' he called. 'Come and find me!'

' ... find me!' Echo said. She stepped into the open, holding out her arms.

Narcissus stared at Echo. 'Who are you?'
he said. 'I wasn't looking for *you.*'

' ... looking for *you*!' Echo whispered.
She reached out and tried to hug him.

Narcissus pulled a face and backed away
from her. 'Don't touch me!' he said.

' ... touch me!' pleaded Echo.

Narcissus looked at her in horror. 'No!'
he shouted. 'Leave me alone!' He turned
and ran away, as fast as he could.

' ... alone!' wailed Echo, running after him.
But she couldn't keep up. Narcissus
vanished into the trees and all
she could do was follow his
tracks, hoping to find
him again.

She didn't eat. She didn't sleep. She was
too much in love to do anything except run
after Narcissus. Slowly she faded away until
there was nothing left of her. Except
her voice.

Narcissus went on running for a long time. As he ran, he shouted, again and again, hoping to find his friends. But no one answered and soon he was completely lost.

At last he came to a clearing in the forest. The grass was soft and green and there was a pool of clear, still water in the middle of the clearing.

Narcissus was very tired and very, very thirsty. He knelt beside the pool and bent down to scoop up some water. But before his hand broke the surface of the water he saw a face down there, looking back at him.

It was so beautiful that he almost stopped breathing.

Narcissus stared down at the beautiful face in the water.

'Who are you?' he whispered.

The lovely face seemed to speak back to him, but there was no sound. He saw its lips moving, but he couldn't work out what they were saying.

'Please come out of the water!' he begged. 'You are the most beautiful thing I have ever seen. I love you!'

The lips under the water moved as he spoke. It looked as though they were saying, 'I love you.' Joyfully, Narcissus reached down into the pool, trying to catch hold of the face and pull it towards him. But the water broke up into ripples and the face disappeared completely.

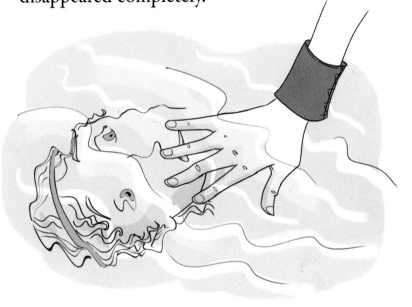

At last Narcissus understood. There was no other, beautiful person under the water. The face he could see was his own reflection.

'What shall I do?' he cried. 'I've fallen in love – with myself!'

That just made him feel more hopeless. He couldn't drag himself away. He lay beside the pool, gazing down at his reflection, full of sadness and longing. Sometimes he wept, but when his tears fell into the water the reflection broke up and the face disappeared again.

Slowly his strength melted away, like wax melting in a flame. Like frost melting in the heat of the sun. He couldn't eat. He couldn't sleep. All he could do was gaze at the face in the water.

That is how he was when Echo found him at last. The moment she saw him, she knew he was very near death.

'Alas,' he was saying as he stared down into the water. 'Alas, alas.'

' ... alas!' whispered Echo.

'I am going to die,' Narcissus told his reflection. 'I love you, more than anything, but this is the end.' He lowered his head onto the grass. 'I have to say goodbye.'

' ... goodbye,' murmured Echo, as his eyes closed.

She watched until Narcissus's friends came looking for him. But there was no body for them to bury. All they found was a beautiful new flower, with a circle of white petals around a yellow centre. Its head was bent, facing down towards its own reflection in the water.

We call that flower a narcissus.

And what happened to Echo? She still wanders around in forests and caves. Or you might find her near a cliff, or in some lonely place in the mountains. Sometimes, if you walk there, you can hear her calling back to you.

... calling back to you ...

Arachne[2]

Once upon a time there was a girl called Arachne. Her mother was dead and she lived with her father in a little village in the hills. Her father earned his living by dyeing wool purple, for other people to spin into thread.

[2] say 'uh-rak-nee'

Arachne was the best spinner of all.
The thread she made was fine and long
and strong. She could weave the best cloth
too. And she did it so gracefully that
people from miles around came to watch
her working.

The wood nymphs crept down from
the mountains and the water nymphs came
up from the river, to stare at Arachne
spinning with her spindle and weaving on
the loom in her cottage.

The cloth she made was so lovely that people started wondering how she had learned to weave like that.

'She must have been taught by one of the gods,' they whispered. 'Maybe it was Minerva herself, goddess of all the arts.'

That was a huge compliment. But Arachne didn't think so. When she heard what they were saying, she flew into a temper.

'No one taught me to weave!' she said.
'I taught myself! That's why I'm the best
weaver there has ever been. Even Minerva
can't make cloth like mine.'

That was a shocking thing to say. People
were horrified. But Arachne was too proud
to care.

'If Minerva thinks she can do better than
me – let her prove it,' she said. 'I challenge
her to a weaving competition!'

When Minerva heard Arachne boasting, she was furious.

'That girl must be taught a lesson!' she said.

She disguised herself as an old woman, with grey hair and sunken cheeks, and tottered into Arachne's village, leaning on a stick.

Arachne was outside her father's house, spinning and listening to people praise her work. Minerva watched for a few moments and then spoke to her gently, croaking like an old woman.

'Child, you spin well,' the old woman said. 'And what lovely cloth you have made. I can see why people call you the best weaver in the world. Be happy with that. But don't set yourself against the gods. Apologize to Minerva for challenging her.'

Arachne scowled. 'Why should I apologize? I *am* the best. If you can't see that, then old age has made you stupid. I don't need your advice. Go home and bother your own daughters.'

'Be careful,' Minerva croaked in her old woman's voice. 'It's foolish to anger the gods.'

Arachne tossed her head. 'If Minerva thinks her weaving is better than mine, why doesn't she take up my challenge?'

'I will!' cried Minerva. And she threw off her disguise and blazed out in her full splendour.

The people around Arachne were terrified. They all fell to their knees in front of the goddess. But Arachne didn't. She stood tall, staring back at Minerva, and her face was pink with excitement. This was the moment she had been longing for. This was her chance to prove she was better than the gods.

'Let the competition begin!' she said.

Arachne and Minerva marched into the house side by side. They set up their looms in different corners, stretching out the long warp threads. Then they loaded their shuttles with lots of different-coloured wool – and they began to weave.

People crowded round, watching in excitement as the shuttles flew backwards and forwards. As the pieces of cloth grew longer, pictures started forming.

Minerva's tapestry showed her famous race against Neptune, the god of the sea. Neptune had planned to capture the city of Athens, by flooding it. But Minerva reached the city first and struck the hill in the middle of the city with her shining spear. A huge olive tree sprang up there – and the city was hers.

She wove the whole story. And in the four corners of the tapestry she wove four other scenes, as a terrible warning to Arachne. There were two mountains, a crane with its wings flapping, a stork, and a flight of steps. All these had once been people – until they dared to set themselves against the gods.

Minerva finished her tapestry with a border of olives, the sign of peace. Then she went to see what Arachne had woven.

Arachne had woven a different picture of the gods. In her tapestry, they were not splendid and victorious. She had chosen stories where they changed into animal shapes, to trick human beings. In one scene, Jupiter was a bull. In others he was a swan, and a snake.

Neptune was there too, disguised as a ram in one place and a horse in another, and Phoebus,[3] the sun god, was shown as a lion. In some pictures, the gods were not even animals. Jupiter was a shower of gold and Bacchus[4] was a bunch of grapes.

Arachne's tapestry was perfectly woven and her pictures were even more beautiful than Minerva's. But every one of them made the gods look wicked and foolish.

The goddess Minerva exploded into a fierce rage.

[3] say 'fee-buss'   [4] say 'ba-kuss'

Pulling Arachne's tapestry off the loom,
Minerva tore it into a thousand pieces.
Then, with her shuttle, she hit Arachne on
the forehead, four times.

Now Arachne understood how stupid
she had been. How could she go on living
if Minerva was angry with her? She was
terrified.

'My life is over!' she wailed in despair.
'Let me die now!'

When Minerva heard that, she took pity on Arachne – in a way.

'No,' she said. 'Go on living – and spinning. But in another shape.'

She reached out her hand and sprinkled Arachne with juice from a magic herb. At once, Arachne began to change. All her hair fell out. Her ears disappeared and her head shrank, until it was almost too small to see.

The top of her body shrank too. And her fingers, all eight of them, changed into tiny legs and fixed themselves along the sides of her shrunken body. Below that, her belly swelled out. Now it was the biggest part of her.

With one hand, Minerva lifted her up and dropped her onto the roof beam.

'Hang there,' she said, 'and go on spinning for ever – you and your children and your children's children.'

There was no
answer from Arachne.
She just went on
spinning and spinning,
the finest, most
delicate thread in the
world. But she never
wove another
picture.

Because she had changed into a spider.

Baucis and Philemon[5]

Far away in the hills, there were once two ancient trees. One was an oak and the other was a lime tree and they grew very close together. Around them, the land was marshy and wild and no one lived there except birds and water creatures.

This is the story of those two trees.

[5] say 'bor-sis and fil-ee-mun'

The place where they grew was once good farmland, dotted with little houses. Thousands of people lived there, working on the land and growing food for themselves. They had good lives, but they were thoughtless and selfish.

One day, Jupiter and Mercury came down from Mount Olympus, the home of the gods. They disguised themselves as poor travellers and went from house to house, knocking on every door.

'We are tired and hungry,' they called. 'We need something to eat and a place to sleep. Will you help us?'

But in every house the doors were bolted and barred. No one asked them in or gave them any food.

At last, they came to a very small cottage, thatched with reeds. It was the home of an old woman called Baucis and her husband, Philemon. They had no servants and hardly any money, but they didn't worry about being poor. They were very happy together.

There was a big old goose in their garden. As Jupiter and Mercury walked up to the cottage door, the goose cackled loudly. Before Jupiter could knock, Baucis had opened the door wide, with a warm smile on her face.

'Come in, come in!' she said. 'It's getting late and you look tired and hungry.'

Baucis put more wood on the fire and it blazed up brightly, warming the whole house. She pulled two chairs up close to the fire.

'Sit here and get the chill out of your bones,' she said to Jupiter and Mercury. 'My husband and I will make you some supper.'

Philemon was already out in their little garden, digging up vegetables. When he brought them in, Baucis started cooking straight away.

Philemon lifted down the piece of meat
that was hanging over the fire to smoke. It
was all they had, but he cut off thick slices
for their visitors and gave them to Baucis
to cook.

As they worked, the two old people
chatted to Jupiter and Mercury, making
them feel welcome. And when the meal was
ready, Baucis fetched the table and set it
down in front of the fire.

It was a very old table and she had to put a piece of tile under one leg to stop it wobbling, but it was clean and well polished. The wooden cups she put out were polished too.

'You must be thirsty,' she said. 'Please drink.'

She picked up her old pottery jug and filled the cups.

Baucis laid out cherries and radishes on the table, with a piece of cheese and some roasted eggs. When Jupiter and Mercury had finished those, she served the stew she had cooked. And after the stew she gave them a basket of fruit and a big piece of honeycomb.

She had made the very best meal she could, and she smiled as she watched her visitors eating.

Then she and Philemon noticed something strange.

Strange and frightening.

The two visitors had been drinking thirstily. Every time their cups were empty, Baucis lifted her old pottery jug and filled them again.

And again.

And again.

And the jug was never empty. *It kept filling itself again.*

When Baucis and Philemon realized what was happening, they knew what it meant. Their visitors were not ordinary travellers. *They were gods.*

The two old people were terrified. They had gods in their house – and they had been treating them like ordinary people.

'Please forgive us,' said Baucis, 'for giving you such a poor meal!'

'We'll fetch something better!' said Philemon.

They rushed out of the house together and started chasing the old goose in their garden.

They loved that goose. It gave them
eggs and warned them when visitors were
coming. But they had nothing else left to
give the gods. They had to catch the goose!

The goose was big and strong and
Baucis and Philemon were old and slow.
Before they could catch it, it had raced into
the house. They ran after it and found it
standing next to Jupiter, with its head
on his knees.

'Don't kill it,' Jupiter said. 'You've already given us a fine meal. Just come with us – as fast as you can. You're the only good people in this wicked place.'

He led them outside. Behind the house was a steep mountain. He started up the slope and Baucis and Philemon struggled after him, leaning on their sticks.

Before they reached the top, they heard a strange gurgling, squelching sound. They turned round – and burst into tears.

While they were climbing, the valley below them had flooded. All the houses had disappeared – except one – and all the people were drowned. The only house left was their own little cottage.

And even that was changing. As they watched, the old wooden walls became fine marble. The rickety doors grew solid and tall, covered in beautiful carvings. And the thatched roof turned gleaming yellow, shining so brightly they knew it had to be made of gold.

Their poor little house had changed into a beautiful temple.

Jupiter looked at them. 'You are good people,' he said. 'What would you like me to do for you?'

Baucis and Philemon talked quietly for a moment. Then Philemon said, 'We want to live in your temple and serve you for the rest of our lives. And, when we die, let us both die at the very same moment. Then neither of us will have to see the other's funeral.'

'Your wishes are granted,' Jupiter said.
'Live and be happy.'

And so they did. They lived in the temple
for the rest of their lives, until they were
very, very old.

One day, they were standing by the temple steps together, talking about how the gods had visited them. Suddenly, Baucis saw leaves sprouting from Philemon's shoulders. At the same moment, Philemon saw Baucis's fingers growing long as they changed into twigs.

They knew they had reached the
end of their human lives. As
their bodies stiffened and
bark crept up their legs,
they called out
to each other,
at the very
same moment.

'Goodbye, my dearest one! Goodbye!'
A second later, there was no old man
by the steps. And no old woman either.
Where Philemon had stood, there was a
tall and stately oak tree. And beside him,
where Baucis had been, was a lime tree with
beautiful heart-shaped leaves.

Ovid and the *Metamorphoses*

Ovid was a poet from Ancient Rome, born in 43 BCE. *Metamorphoses* is one of his most famous poems. Its title means 'changing shape' and it is a collection of stories about people transforming into other things, like animals and stars.

Ovid did not invent the stories – some are ancient myths and some are legends about real people, like Julius Caesar. Ovid joined the stories up to make a fantasy history of the world.

While Ovid was still writing the poem, the Emperor Augustus banished him from Rome. No one is quite sure why, but it was a serious punishment. Ovid flew into a rage and threw *Metamorphoses* into a fire.

Luckily, there were other copies and the poem survives for us to enjoy, two thousand years later.